WONDERCRUMP POETRY!

The best children's poems
from the
Roald Dahl
Poetry Competition,
1994

Edited by Jennifer Curry

A Red Fox Book

Published by Random House Children's Books
20 Vauxhall Bridge Road, London SW1V 2SA

A division of Random House UK Ltd
London Melbourne Sydney Auckland
Johannesburg and agencies throughout the world

Copyright © text Random House Children's Books 1995
Designed by Ness Wood

1 3 5 7 9 10 8 6 4 2

First published by Red Fox 1995

Set in Janson by Intype, London
Printed and bound in Great Britain by
The Guernsey Press Co. Ltd, Guernsey, Channel Islands

RANDOM HOUSE UK Limited Reg. No. 954009

ISBN 0 09 952261 6

Contents

Introduction

It seemed like a *mountain*, the mass of poetry that was submitted to the competition. The mountain consisted of thousands of pieces of paper, which had to be reduced to approximately 160 poems to fit into one small book. For months we sifted and considered every contribution.

So, what were we looking for in our deliberations? We were *not* searching primarily for sophisticated form and structure or complex rhyme schemes. When we did find these we were pleased, but many of our poets are too inexperienced to have achieved technical excellence. (Our youngest is four-year-old Alex Coburn.) We *were* searching for the child's personal vision of life, for images that sprang fresh from his or her imagination – and not the teacher's – and for a use of words and clarity of description that leapt off the page (take Amy Tullett's poem, for example. I can't look at a fire extinguisher now without seeing it through new eyes). We were also seeking that quality of compression, of tautness and disciplined management of language, that distinguishes poetry from prose.

All these we found, and more. We were given an inside view of what it is like to be growing up in Britain today. These young writers make sense of their lives by turning them into stories. Through the stories they tell *us*, we can understand *them*. In their work we find courage, wit, joy, grief, love, excitement, anger, hope, laughter and desolation. Who can fail to be moved by Andre Pears' account of the very moment when, at the age of four, he went deaf, 'buzzing on the handles like a bee'? Or by Mairi Hall's funny, brave account of her experience of scoliosis? Who can not recognize Jackson Ingle's sadness at feeling like 'the smallest potato in the plastic bag'?

But there is joy here too, and a vigorous – and invigorating – commitment to life, expressed in language that sings. 'The sun is a cupcake,' declares Catherine Garnett, while Amanda Rose remembers 'the welly-squelch of autumn' and Charlotte Castro greets the beginning of summer, 'We exploded from school/Like racehorses out to grass./ We galloped into the hideouts . . .' For sheer bravado, though, I salute Rebecca Evans who vividly voices a desire every grown woman remembers. 'I am 12 and a half and I'd like to grow some breasts./ I would love to wear a bra because I'm sick of wearing vests.'

From this plethora of talent we had to choose one Poet of the Year. Each judge made a nomination, four candidates were asked to send us three more poems, in haste, and the final decision was made on the basis of their complete dossiers. Our choice of Rachel Barrett was unanimous. Her work has a mature discipline and control, she is able to write with great restraint about difficult and emotive issues, and she is not afraid to tackle a variety of subject matter, style and mood.

Our two winning schools, Handford Hall County Primary and Wimbledon High, gained highest points because practically *all* the poems they submitted were interesting and original, and they offered a broad range of subjects, deftly handled. We were particularly delighted that the School Of the Year turned out to be a *primary* school.

1994 was a good year for children's poetry. For me, it was a delight to judge and select these poems. I hope it will be a delight for you to read them.

Jennifer Curry

Jennifer Curry – Chair of the Judging Panel
Wondercrump Winners

Wondercrump Winners

Poet of the Year
Rachel Barrett
Debenham High School
Stowmarket, Suffolk

School of the Year
Handford Hall County Primary
Ipswich, Suffolk

Wondercrump Poetry Award
Wimbledon High School
Wimbledon, London

Age Category Winners
Age 7 and under
Nadia Hamidi
Southbank International School, London
Billy Ward
Alverton County Primary School, Penzance, Cornwall
Merve Escobedo
Southbank International School, London
Patrick Anderson
Handford Hall County Primary, Ipswich, Suffolk
Benji Inwood
Darell School, Richmond, Surrey
Ellie Thomson
Handford Hall County Primary, Ipswich, Suffolk

Age 8–11

Caroline Allen
Wimbledon High School, London
Barney Waite
Darell School, Richmond, Surrey
Laura Middlewick
Handford Hall County Primary, Ipswich, Suffolk
Katie McDermott
Glenola Collegiate, Bangor, County Down
James Mathieson
Ponteland County Middle School, Newcastle Upon Tyne,

Tyne and Wear

Amy Tullet
Heyworth County Primary School, Haywards Heath, West Sussex

Age 12–14

Zoe Layton
St Nicholas School, Harlow, Essex
Sarah Hunter
Debenham High School, Stowmarket, Suffolk
Daniel Ribenfors
Halesworth Middle School, Halesworth, Suffolk
Eleanor Borer
Halesworth Middle School, Halesworth, Suffolk
Leila Anani
Debenham High School, Stowmarket, Suffolk
Gail Trimble
The Lady Eleanor Holles School, Hampton, Middlesex

Age 15–17

Sarah Farthing
Debenham High School, Stowmarket, Suffolk
Sarah Stringer
St Bede's School, Redhill, Surrey

Ruth Taylor
Chester, Cheshire
Cheryl May Thompson
Teeside High School, Stockton-on-Tees, Cleveland
Lucy Howard
Wimbledon High School, London
Efchi Michalacopoulos
London

A STORY LOST IN A LIBRARY

(First words)

There is in me

There is in me
a hedgehog that snuffles through
leaves looking for friends.
There is in me
ballet music from Swan Lake
played on an empty stage at midnight.
There is in me
soft snow
melting in country brooks.
There is in me
a mouse that scuttles in
dustbins for scraps.
There is in me
the gentle waves
of the sea.
There is in me
a story
lost in a library.

Alice Pyper (8)
Handford Hall Primary School
Ipswich, Suffolk
(School of the Year)

DEEP INSIDE ME
(poems about myself)

Me

I hope they see that
I am what I am inside,
Not outside.
If they only saw
The wreck above the mine,
Rusty metal buildings,
Mountains on the ground
Where the mud has been,
They might turn away.

But I am what I am inside.
They might find some
treasure.
Diamonds glittering,
Gold shining,
Deep inside me,
If they dig hard enough,
And long enough.

I am what I am inside.
Not what I couldn't be
Outside.

Ben Samuel (10)
Darell School
Richmond, Surrey

The writer of this poem

The writer of this poem
Is stronger than an ox,
As sparkling as a diamond
As cunning as a fox.

As glamorous as a film-star
As bright as the sun,
As exciting as a circus
As clever as they come.

As healthy as a vegetable
As busy as a bee
As valuable as an emerald
As wonderful as the sea.

The writer of this poem
Is purer than a pearl
As brave as a lion
But not a modest girl!

Sarah Lattimore (13)
Brentwood Ursuline Convent
Essex

Motorbike mad

They call me Harley.
Man, Ah'm cool!
Ah'm jest a
Motorcyclin' fool.

Ah'm eight years old,
Ah'm tough as boots,
Ah like studs
An' leather suits.

Ah'm so hot
Ah almos' boil!
Ah grease mah hair
With engine oil!

In life Ah need:
Mah bike,
The open road,
And speed!

Mah mum's a biker,
Dad's one too
So what's a kid
Supposed to do?

To motorcyclin'
Ah was drawn—
A biker isn't made—
He's born!

James Mathieson (11)
Ponteland County Middle School
Newcastle-upon-Tyne
(Age Category Winner)

The rainy window

Rain sliding down glass
Mixing the garden colours
My eyes start to smile

Nadia Hamidi (6)
Southbank International School
London
(Age Category Winner)

Happiness

I jump, skip, run and play
When I'm happy every day.
I laugh with my friends
And play some games.
I play with my blackboard
and roller blades.
I like to see a happy race
With broad smiles and sparkling eyes.
The world would be
A better place
If everyone had happiness.

Gemma Boyd (7)
Newbuilding Primary School
Londonderry, Northern Ireland

Spaghetti Bolognaise

Spaghetti Bolognaise, Spaghetti Bolognaise,
I love, I love Spaghetti Bolognaise.
Mince in the middle, Spaghetti round the ledge,
Sauce with the mince, Spaghetti off the edge.
Spaghetti Bolognaise, Spaghetti Bolognaise,
I love, I love Spaghetti Bolognaise.

Hannah Bush (9)
Brambletye Junior School
Redhill, Surrey

The skiver's rhyme

I was ill yesterday,
I was ill the day before,
She thinks I'm ill today,
But I'm not ill anymore.

Elizabeth Wardle (12)
St Gregory's R.C. High School
Warrington, Cheshire

A-choo!

You can feel it coming,
That tickle in your nose,
That shiver up your spine,
That tingle in your toes.
You do not have a tissue,
Oh no! what can you do?
Prepare for an explosion –
A-CHOO!

Danielle Meinrath (9)
Channing School
Highgate, London

Memories

The azure blue sky
reflecting from the sea.
The warmth of the sun
shimmering on the water.

These are my memories.

The tall grey mountains
standing as if they were dead.
The buildings were cool
and comfortable.

These are my memories.

The restaurant was big and busy.
The strange new smells,
the taste of foods.
All mysterious and new to me.

These are my memories.

The friendly atmosphere
surrounded me.
The people were kind and helpful.
Everywhere I went
a welcome awaited me.

These are my memories.

The swimming pool was warm,
and crowded.
The laughter of people,
filled the air.

These are my memories.

The facilities were fun to use.
They were there to amuse.
The shops with plenty of choice,
expensive though they were.

These are my memories.

The soft warm sand,
with hiding stones,
and the hard hot ground
that burnt my feet.

These are my memories.

The cats were waiting to be fed,
sitting patiently for food to drop.
The insects buzzed around the tables,
disturbing me as I ate.

THESE ARE MY MEMORIES.

Justin Chainey (10)
Stanmore

Hostel drying room

Exhausted,
I push at the door marked
'Drying Room'.
Wrapped like a sheep,
I stumble inside,
My shivering subsiding
As the hot air strokes my face.

Socks, hats and scarves
Tangle in a maze of hangers and pipes.
A coat drips
And everything hangs cloudy,
Heavy, wet, dark and lonely,
Breathing in the thick air.
I sink down in a corner,
Piled high with boots,
And imagine
Their collection of trodden memories.
I hope that tomorrow
The sun will emerge
With a shock to the landscape
And take me home with happiness.
But I know this dingy drying room
Is to me
A momentary comfort
In a cold, cold world.

Abbi Lock (15)
Debenham High School
Stowmarket, Suffolk

Scoli and me (Scoliosis)

Blue hat, like a shower cap.
Coming to take off the magic cream,
Going to have some sort of dream.

Black in my eyes,
Petrified!
The ventilator's caught in my throat.
Trying to swallow.
Can't speak my sorrow,
But Mum understands.

People and cameras,
All over the place.
On TV they're going to show my face.
It's a new thing,
I'm controlling my pain
With a button that delivers morphine.

Orange and yellow,
A window by my side.
Like coming home to Mum and Gran,
Still woozy and sleepy,
On the stryker frame,
Like a roll of tuna and mayonnaise,
I'm sandwiched between two mattresses.
One minute I'm here, looking at the ceiling,
The next I'm there. What a funny feeling!
Looking at the floor.

Ten days later
I was plastered.
Mr Wilson was playing classical bands
While Yvonne was being artistic with her
scissorhands.
A jacket from my neck to my hip
Feeling dark blue 'cos it's giving me jip!

Sister Gilchrist adjusts it

Mairi Hall (11)
Kilmarnock, Scotland

Underground train

It roars through the tunnel,
A monster growling and rushing,
Its hot breath blows out,
Lifting my skirt,
And it's a fight to hold it down.
Lights beam out like shining eyes,
It squeals to a halt,
Its doors open wide and swallow me up.

Ellen Coffey (7)
Handford Hall Primary School
Ipswich, Suffolk
(School of the Year)

Visiting time

The big doors opened on
That smell –
A mixture of old people's hair
And urine.
The television was the only life,
Squealing of sensible shoes,
And the constant thud
Of laboured breathing
Echoed faintly.
We entered the room.
I saw him
Sitting,
Breathing,
Hearing,
Watching.
I sat down beside him
And grasped his hand.
His wrinkled neck turned.
I leaned forward
And kissed him.
He smiled.
'I got you some oranges,'

Mum said conversationally.
I looked down at my pleated skirt,
Specially picked for today.
I was seven when he became ill.
I'd always wanted to sit,
Watch and
Listen.
The day had finally come.
I was excited.
The adult tension in the air
Was too far away
For me to grab
And understand.

Victoria Walker (14)
Debenham High School
Stowmarket, Suffolk

Money

The things I could buy with it,
The people who would beg for it,
Money,
I like that stuff.

The places I could go with it,
The people I could meet with it,
Money,
I like that stuff.

The wildlife I could save with it,
The people I could help with it,
Money,
I like that stuff.

The lives that are lost for it,
The greedy minds that lust for it,
Money,
I hate that stuff.

Jason Rae (13)
Merchant Taylors Boys' School
Merseyside

The cathedral

Quiet, still, silent,
Candles surround us,
People praying,
Dull,
Chilly but not cold,
Echoing sounds as people walk,
Step, step, step, on the uncovered stone floor.

Lights set up around it,
Speakers around,
Want to run,
Want to shout,
Something stops you though,
Strange but compelling.

Stuart Greenwood (11)
Georgian Gardens Primary
Rustington, West Sussex

Learning the violin

He gave me an hourglass figure,
The bridge suspending her tiny sound box.
He tuned her,
A slightly Chinese sound sliding, scaling the notes,
As he turned the pegs.

He towered over me,
And the hairs in his nose quavered,
Like the open D string.

I looked at the music.
There was a picture: a teddy bear combing his hair:
'Teddy bear is very good.
He knows the things that he should . . . do!'
I played and Mr Griffiths sang.

She came to life as I plucked the string.
Her stillness was shattered,
As vibrations echoed round the room.

She sounded like a gramophone
Playing 'English Country Garden'
On a scratchy record.

I practised and practised,
Then put her to bed.
And closed her case.

Daisy Cooper (12)
Halesworth Middle School
Suffolk

Knees

I like knees,
bony knees,
wobbly knees,
itchy knees,
neat knees.
I like knees,
bruised knees,
praying knees,
knees with honey on,
knees with jam on,
    knees
    knees
    knees.

Katie Wilson (6)
Binfield C of E Primary School
Bracknell, Berks

Computer explosion

I'll remember the day
my computer blew up and
blasted everything
on that programme
into mid-air.
15 + 20 = 39 instead of 35?......dislocation!
Oxygen being breathed in by trees
and out by humans?
Carbon dioxide being breathed in
by humans and out by plants?
Words mixing up . . .
Story Writing became
Wory Stiting
NOTHING WAS GOING RIGHT!!
I looked outside,
a cat was walking
upside down, hanging
from the top branch
of a tree........
THE WILDEST DREAMS
BEYOND MY IMAGINATION!!!
I pressed ESCAPE.
First a fizzing noise
and then a BANG!..........
The programme was gone,
lost forever,
but everything was

back to normal.
I looked outside,
I saw that cat
only lying dazed,
on the branch below.
I was inhaling oxygen and
exhaling carbon dioxide
once again.
How can I forget the day
my computer blew up?

Dionysios Georgiou (8)
Kingsgate Junior School
London

My poem

The day I went deaf when I was four.
Before I went deaf I could hear lorries going past my
house.
When I was in bed they rumbled by.
In the morning, I could hear birds.
They were singing and twittering.
I could hear my mother and father speak and shout at me,
When they were talking to me or when I did something
wrong.
But when I went deaf, I couldn't.

The minute I went deaf
I was hanging on the door handles with my hands.
My ears went POP.
Like the pop on cling film when you blow it up and
squash it.
Then my mum spoke to me.
It was total silence.
It was like my ears had vandals and they destroyed
them.
So my mum said, 'Hello, can you hear me?'
I was just buzzing on the handles like a bee.
My mum got up and gave me a tap.
I said, 'What?'
When I said 'what' I couldn't hear my own voice.
So I said, 'I can't hear.'
My mum said, 'Come on don't be silly.'
I said, 'What did you say?'

Andre Pears (14)
William Sharp School - Hearing Impaired Unit
Bilborough, Notts

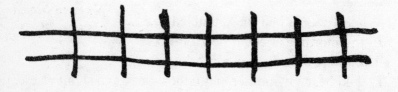

This is how I felt

When he left, I felt confused,
Was it my fault? Why did I feel so alone?
My mum was there, so were my friends,
But he had you.
When I first met you, you were not as I imagined.
I was scared I'd start fighting with you
But much to my surprise, we grew to be like friends.

When you both told me your 'good news',
I was happy for you both – but inside I felt jealous.
Jealous at the fact that I would be left out.
But then you told me it wouldn't change anything.
So when you got sick and lost the baby
I really did feel sad. Angry at myself and sad for you both.
I know you are still hurting – I hope time will heal
the pain.

Emma Brown (15)
Enniskillen High School
Co. Fermanagh,
Northern Ireland

Mary

My friend and I have broken up,
Broken up over a girl.
He has built up walls between us.
I knock one down,
He builds another.
I try to talk sense,
He turns away.
I knock down a wall,
He builds another.
I say, 'Let's have a contest, and see who wins.'
'OK,' he says.
'The winner gets Mary.'
We have an arm wrestling contest.
He wins.
I say, 'That's not fair.'
He builds a wall.
I can't knock it down.

Mark Richard Nathan (12)
St John's School
Northwood, Middlesex

The Tate Gallery

(After seeing Dennis Mitchell's work)

Shiny sword in the air,
Made of bronze,
Standing in the gallery.
Beautiful and quiet,
Not a sound.
Standing as still as a house.
The sword said, 'leave me alone,
or else I'll chop your head off!!
and I'll blind you with my shine.
Leave me alone!! Leave me alone!!
Leave me alone!! Leave me alone!!'

Billy Ward (7)
Alverton County Primary
Penzance, Cornwall
(Age Category Winner)

Room

My room is sacred. I have doused a brush
in brine and smeared the walls
in silence. Only the drops dribble
ceaselessly down the distance
of wasteland white, as if
it were a window in bleak
weather, or a memory of eyes in leisure.
Or a mirror.

I have fogged the bulb
that burned too bright, smashed it, left the glass
to do its own dirty work in
shards of sculptured blades below.
Now I keep the lamps
low.
I have drained the coffee cups to
death, constructed shelves to
bear the burden of seventeen years' dust
and filth.
I have torn a strip from the winter,
I have hung it in a corner and
have watched it
wither, like the paper I peeled with my
eyeballs cracked over,
and the socks

that I split with the surgeon's razor.
Only the clock that I crucified to the wall
I pay attention to
at all.

I have traced whispers on the window
with a frozen finger, a wreath
of evening mist to ring her,
quite reasonably; I've room to breathe.
I have slit a small hole in the
ceiling, barely enough to let the
cold come in.
I have carved a bed for bones, too lean
for nights too long to pass in dream, and
worn my joints like crinoline, nurtured
bags beneath my eyes, festered
lies beneath my skin.

Certainly it is no unmethodical practice.
I have raised the grave of a history.
I surround myself with what I know
is familiar, to me.
That echo? It is I, waxing the floor
with footsteps.
That is not a scream. It is the creak of the door.

Robert McColl (17)
Chew Stoke
Nr Bristol

My den

The cobwebs glitter
Like a thousand stars.
They glimmer in the
Night sky.

The earthenware pots
Smell of old earth
Mixed with the dull taste
Of mud.

Suddenly a spider
Runs out from one of the pots
And makes a rustling sound
As it goes.

In the distance I hear
A tractor chugging
As it ploughs great
Furrows in a field.

The old leaves
Feel delicate and frail
To touch. Like the hands
Of an old lady.

Voices in the garden
Fade away,
Leaving only
The croaking of the frogs.

And the cloaks of night
Fold over my den,
Once more a home
To mice.

Henry Wingate (11)
Halesworth Middle School
Suffolk

La

La bume dee, La bume dee
La
This is the tune
The magic maker
Notes plonking on
As Earth twirls.
Spirits of the stars,
Come down
Whispering. Examining
Us followers
Of the braindeadening melody.

Someone! Someone!
Rewrite the scales
Stop life's addictive tapping
On those chords
That control time, and
Timetable pleasures.

Oh glittering magic
Of The Magic Trance Maker
Let me dance free.

Bold Reality
Come rescue me.

Elaine Osewele, (15)
Harlesden, London

Superstar

I WANNA BE A SUPERSTAR,
I wanna drive a massive car,
I wanna join the famous set,
I wanna own a private jet,
I wanna lot of fun at nights,
I wanna name that's up in lights,
I wanna lot of caviare,
I WANNA BE A SUPERSTAR.
I wann applause from near and far,

I wanna private burger bar,
I wanna thrash a flash guitar,
I wanna unlimited supply of coke,
Just like that Phillip Schofield bloke,
I WANNA BE A SUPERSTAR.
I wanna name that should be seen,
I wanna shake hands with the Queen,
I wann the load that fame will buy,
I wanna talk to Princess Di,
I wanna be better than you,
I wanna talk to Prince Charles, too
I WANNA BE A SUPERSTAR

On second thoughts,
Now let me see,
I think I'm better off
As me.

Amieth Yogarajah (9)
Mount Stewart Juniors
Kenton, Middlesex

My tree

Private place, private thoughts . . .

It's quiet – well, apart from the starlings squabbling,
The combine harvester at work in the field,
The children playing in the nearby garden.
I can't really hear them.
I'm thinking, thinking.

I can smell the new-mown grass.
Someone's lunch is wafting my way. It makes my
tummy rumble.
Still I sit on, thinking, thinking.

Gently my fingers brush the bark.
The sap sticks to my hand and smells of honey.
But still I sit, thinking, thinking.

I wriggle around, try to get more cosy.
My friends reach my thinking:
'I can see you!'
'Caught you!'
'Where's James?'
Quickly, I climb down from my private tree
And stop my thinking, thinking, thinking!

Philip Clark (11)
Halesworth Middle School
Suffolk

HELLO, MUM IT'S ME
(poems of family and home)

Memories

The big old house
Still smells of her,
Everything left how it was.
Then in we come,
Black bags rustling.

Sixteen bin liners,
Sixteen black bags
Full of her life,
Waiting,
Waiting.

Memories rekindled,
Presents given,
Taken back.

A house left
Empty,
But full with memories,
For a new family,
New memories,
New life.

Clare Nicholls (15)
Robertsbridge Community College
Robertsbridge, East Sussex

The Thurlow Arms

A chatter of low voices,
A smell of people smoking.
The thump of a dart hitting its target.
A bell rings behind the bar,
Heat emerges from the kitchen.
Some water runs down the sink.
And Doily the dog barks.
The noise of the ping-pong machine,
And the crackling, welcoming, glowing fire.
The creaking of a big, wooden door,
And a car pulls away outside.
All of these sounds,
All of these smells,
And all of these thoughts,
Make the pleasant and friendly feel of a pub,
Where I live.

Holly Welch (10)
William Cobbett Junior School
Farnham, Surrey

Our house

It's really weird at our house.
Mum's a walking book.
Dad's as quiet as a mouse,
My brother's a crazy cook.

Grandma's a humpback vampire,
Grandpa's legs are hooks.
A guy fawkes on a bonfire
is Uncle's latest look.

Aunty's a six-foot blood clot
My cousin's as deaf as a post
But I'm the scariest of the lot,
I'm a walking, talking GHOST!

Jenny Walker (11)
Catshill Middle School
Bromsgrove, Worcestershire

A full moon

I lie on my bed in the dead of the night,
The whole house is silent, not a person in sight.
The eerie glow of the Take-Away from across the street
Creeps under my blind, and dances on my feet.
My wardrobe's jaws are open wide,
Ready to trap any brave hero inside,
To crunch him up with his coat-hanger teeth,
And swallow down into his cupboards beneath.

My eyelids slowly drop, I'm nearly asleep,
The wardrobe has stopped munching,
The lights have ceased to creep.
But what I didn't notice, until it was too late,
My school shirts upon the floor
Had begun to rise and shake.
They danced around my bedroom,
They wobbled on my desk.
One bold, bold shirt even asked
For a dance with my school dress.

Katie McDermott (11)
Glenola Collegiate Preparatory Dept.,
Bangor, County Down
(Age Category Winner)

Colours

My Dad wears a red jumper
He looks happy and bright.

My Mum wears a blue uniform
She works at night.

My brother has a green track suit
He wears it for fun.

I wear a white T-shirt
It's cool in the sun.

Reilly wears yellow socks
Which make him feel hot.

But green is, for me,
the best of the lot.

Amie Moule (7) and friends
Heyworth County Primary
Haywards Heath, West Sussex

But it was silent in the car behind

There was Rock and Roll music in the car in front,
But it was silent in the car behind.

Kids were screaming in the car in front,
But it was silent in the car behind.

Mums were shouting to get the children quiet in the
car in front,
But it was silent in the car behind.

Dogs were barking in the car in front,
But it was silent in the car behind.

A ball made a dent in the car in front,
But it was silent in the car behind.

The mothers and children and dogs tumbled out of
the car in front for a picnic in the park,
And the little girl in the car behind thought, 'I wish
I was in the car in front!'

Maisie Baynham (6)
Stourbridge, West Midlands

The boring bonfire

Is that the bonfire?
Surely not.
It looks, well, sort of small.
All that wood.
All that time collecting it.
I expected it to be huge, towering above me
menacing.
I can see shapes in the twisted boughs and branches,
Strange shapes, weird shapes, faces of unnamed
animals.
All the people who want to see it
Will never be as disappointed as me,
I think I'll go home now,
And tell my mother not to bother.
I don't want to see it now,
It looks really boring.
My mum makes me go with her.
I told her not to bother,
She told me I would love it.
I really don't see how.
We arrive at the field.
I nearly started to cry.
I decided to sit by the barn
Until it was all over.
Dad lit the boring old thing.

Suddenly I couldn't believe it,
It was massive, exciting, totally thrilling,
It got bigger and bigger, wider and wider,
I liked last night and I'm glad I went.

Robert Matthew Ellison (10)
Stamford Bridge County Primary School
Stamford Bridge, Nr York

Changes

There were four in the house,
Then suddenly there were six!
Jenny and Kimberley moved in.
Lots of boxes everywhere.

Where would they sleep?
Where would it all go?
Weeks of muddles
Then everything sorted out
And everyone happy.
Eating Jenny's sausage casserole!

Lisa Nash (7)
Hareclive Primary School.
Hartcliffe, Bristol

After Christmas - after Hiawatha

In the time of the mid-winter,
In the time of damp and darkness,
When the dreaded term has ended,
Comes the festival of Yuletide.
This the time of Father Christmas,
And of Christmas trees and tinsel.
This the time of seeing Santas,
And of visits to the pantos.
Houses dressed in decorations,
Shine their lights out on the pavements.
        As the advent candles dwindle,
Then the tribes begin to gather,
From across the Great Sea-Water,
From all corners of the Nation;
Ancestors and distant in-laws,
Uncles, Aunts and squabbling cousins.
Sumptuous are the meals our Mothers
Make for Christmas celebrations,
That the feast may be more merry.
And the visitors assemble,
Clad in all their richest raiment.

        After all the noisy talking,
All the laughter and the singing,

After all the overeating,
Snoozing after lunch-time boozing,
When the tribes have long departed,
Comes the voice of the Great Mother:
'HAVE YOU DONE YOUR THANK YOU
LETTERS?'
'But we want to watch the telly,
It is "Neighbours" in five minutes!'
'Do I have to?' whine the children,
'We'll be seeing them on Monday!'
'I'll be ringing her on Sunday!'
'I can do them all tomorrow!'
Wail the children with great sorrow.
        'Finish all this endless talking!
And sit down and get it done with.
Remember that if you don't do them,
There will be no presents next year!'
Then the mind begins to ponder,
'Are those presents what I wanted?
Baby books and frilly panties,
From adoring silly Aunties?
Better were it to go lacking,
Than to write these ghastly letters!'

        'I will tell you, O my children,
Of the mystery of presents,
How the hankies and the talcum,
Which to you were not so welcome,
Come in useful in the long run;
All the bath salts and the notelets,

All the soap and hats with bobbles,
Can be kept for someone's birthday,
Or next year be distributed,
At Christmas time, amongst your teachers.
Thus the wealth of all the chain stores,
Boots and Harrods, Marks and Spencers,
Gets dispersed around the nation.'
    So, observing the Great Orders,
Issued from the Mouth of Wisdom,
Which might well not be forthcoming,
If these orders were not heeded,
Duly carried out and finished.
Then the children bow their heads, and,
Meekly bring out pens and paper.
Then a hush falls on the dwelling,
As the children sit, reluctant.
At the table, with their Mother
Standing, watching, every movement,
As they write their Thank You letters.

Charlotte Judith Howden (12)
Wimbledon High School
London
(Roald Dahl Wondercrump School Award)

The bush

Next to my dad's grave
there's a playground,
to make us happy,
and at the far end
there's a bush.
I never go into it.
It's all prickles
with bluebells, daisies
and roses beside it.
Joe went in
the last time we went.
I was scared
because I didn't know
what was in there,
and I didn't know
what was going to
happen to him.

Ellie Thomson (7)
Handford Hall County Primary School
Ipswich, Suffolk.
(Age Category Winner)
(School of the Year)

Bad day

Call Mum from the station,
She won't be too thrilled,
An hour past curfew—
I'm going to get killed.
'Hello, Mum, it's me,
Yes, I know that I'm late,
We'll take the next train,
No, you don't have to wait.'
Train enters the platform.
'Got to go now, Mum, 'bye!'
Run over the bridge.
And sit down with a sigh.
'Have you all done your homework?'
'I've only done half.'
'I don't see what's funny,
Kate, how can you laugh?'
'That's strange, guys, where are we,
Did we pass here before?'
'Oh great, no we didn't,
My head's getting sore.'
'Excuse me, where is this?
It's where!? Oh, right, thanks.
I hope you lot got that
'cause my mind's gone blank.'
'Let's get off next station
And find our way home.'
'I'd better call Mum first,

Anyone see a 'phone?
Hi, Mum, look I'm sorry,
We caught the wrong train.
It's not our fault really,
Wait, I can explain.
Mum, slow down a little,
You're talking too fast.
Hang on, I can't hear you,
A train's going past.
I've run out of change,
See you later, Mum, 'bye!'
She sounded so angry,
I'm going to die.
'Ruth, what did your mum say?
You're grounded? Same here.
I don't think they'll let me
Go out 'til next year.'
'Shall we get a taxi?
I know it'll cost,
But we've got no choice have we?
Let's face it, we're lost.'
'You're all out of money!?
All right then, I'll pay.
I just want to get home—
It's been a bad day.'

Jo Allan (14)
West Byfleet, Surrey

Lost love

Looking at your picture,
You're clutching those tiny blue flowers.
They remind me of you.
Frail, yet blooming with a delicate strength.
You – we – had seemed invincible,
Just the two of us.
Our own private wonder world.
Our own special love.

Memories crowd into my head,
Like shadows inside a forgotten attic.
But, unlike shadows, each one
Carries its own magical light.
You were so confident we could make it
'If we can withstand this,' you said
'We can withstand anything.'
But now you're gone.

I recall your feelings about life,
Take it, make it, hold on to it.
It's yours, but you only get one chance.
Well, we took it.
Everyone else said it was hopeless
And I should have left you.
But ever since I set eyes on you
I loved you more than life itself.

I treasure our last days together
Like precious jewels in a locked casket
To which only I hold the key.
'When I go, don't look back,' you said.
'I won't.' But I had to
Come just one more time,
To say my last goodbye to you
To finally let you go.

You were an inspiration
To those around you. Your courage
In the face of adversity
Astounded even me.
And so that your memory survives
And your death won't go unheeded
I wrote my last poem to you
My beautiful, wonderful daughter.

Rachel McCluskey (16)
Glossop, Derbyshire

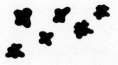

It's so bloody selfish

'It's so bloody selfish!'
They stand on the doorstep.
Haven't bothered to move.
My sister unnoticed between them,
Crying.
Words are slung back and forth.
Broken glass,
Slashing, cutting,
A war of words,
Complete with casualties.
And I watch,
Huddled on the stair,
A confused, frightened bundle
With her first lace-up shoes.
If only they would stop.
Please stop.
Every slither of glass is a theft,
A piece of my world,
Stolen.
A piece of my world,
Desecrated.
Irreplaceable.
It's so bloody selfish.

Rebecca Salt (16)
Thorpe St Andrew High School
Norwich

Old age

Old people's
Skin wrinkles.
Hair grey from brown.
Memories hard to think.
Smoking smoking
in the air.
Smoking smoking
in the air.
A cat called
Scamp,
in a basket.
An outside toilet,
old house,
sitting in her
chair,
Mostly all
day.
Smoking smoking
in the air.
My granny.

Amy Smith (6)
Binfield C of E Primary School
Bracknell, Berkshire

A game of tug and war

I should have got up and shouted.
I should have said something.
I should have had the courage
To stand up and say . . .
'This shouldn't be happening.
You love each other,
You know you do.
I know you do.
Don't do this to yourselves
Or me.'
But I didn't
I said nothing.
Just sat curled up like a snake.
I just sat in the corner.
I swear I was invisible,
The number of times they walked past me.
Just ignoring me.
I may have been small,
But I felt smaller.
The louder the voices.
The smaller I shrank.
I could see them building a wall,
Separating them
From each other.
And I was being left in the middle.
Being pulled at from either side.
Like a game of tug of war,

And I was the rope.
Both teams were determined to win,
But by winning I would lose.
I should have squealed with anger.
I should have stood.
Become the barrier.
Not a weapon to be fought with.
Or a trophy to be awarded to the winner.
But I just sat in the corner
With tears in my eyes.
Curled up like a snake.
Smaller than I was.
But getting smaller still.

Rebecca Woodcock (14)
Baverstock Girls' Middle School
Birmingham

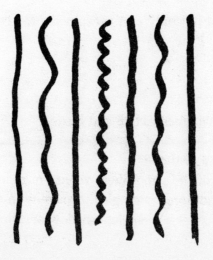

Reign

(Rain)

Standing quietly in the
Rain, lashing my face with vicious
Strength, seeping from my body,
Like pus.

Standing alone in the Reign;—
of my father,
Fearful,
Foreboding.
The pregnant drops fall on my hot cheeks.
Salt—
I realize now not only rain is exploring the contours
of my face,

But also

Tears of unhappiness, Hate and Fear.

The humidity in the air
reminds me of the atmosphere when I'm there,
Standing, smothered, strangled, drowning in the
                        shapeless shadow of The Reign.

Standing quietly in the rain.

Trapped uncomprehendingly
In His Reign.

Louise Amato (14)
The Axe Valley School
Axminster, Devon

Anger is the word always

I am always bored.
I always have to go to school.
I always have tables.
My socks are always smelly.
Things are always the same.
I always want to change them.

Mark Anscombe (7)
Heyworth County Primary School
Haywards Heath, West Sussex

Grandmother

She lay there,
Death alive.
Eighty-nine years for this,
To bleed away.
A benign ancient angel,
Little dignity left,
Except a sleep deep enough
To hide from the world.
Until the slumber is broken,
And death starts to live.
So now she sits and ponders,
Nothing to do,
Nothing to say.
A lively mind
Functioning within an inactive body.
Mumbling of arguments,
Memories,
A life lost.
Waiting for an eternity,
For an end to useless boredom.

Ruth Taylor (16)
Chester, Cheshire

Grandad

Now when I visit Grandad
it isn't quite the same.
I cannot hear him laugh
or joke, or say,
'Can I have a cuppa, mate?'
I cannot watch him read
his books, or do
the football scores.
I cannot hear him say,
'Hello,' anymore.

Now when I visit Grandad,
I kneel and say, 'Hello,'
and place some flowers
on his grave,
hoping that he knows.

Gemma Sadler (8)
Handford Hall County Primary School
Ipswich, Suffolk
(School of the Year)

I remember my dad

I remember his shouts when he was still at home.
I remember the day we rushed him in to hospital.
I remember trying to talk to him when he was in a
coma.

He was my dad,
I remember him, I remember him.

I remember his blue eyes,
I remember his pale brown hair,
I remember his dark clear voice.

He was my dad,
I remember him, I remember him.

I remember his room 'Intensive care',
I was not allowed to see him,
Me and Mum were on our own.

He was my dad,
I remember him, I remember him.

I remember on the Saturday,
I had slept at my Nana's house,
My mum had gone to see him,
(She had brought some bad news).

He was my dad,
I remember him, I remember him.

Mum had some news,
Mum told me and I cried.
Everybody but Mum cried.
She had no tears left in her.

Louise Victoria Voce (9)
Silverhill School, Bristol

Richard

Shouting, screaming, listening, dreaming,
Twiddling, flapping, laughing, clapping,
Always watching, never joining in.
Locked in your world so far away,
The boy in the playground who cannot play.
With no social grace you like to grimace
And make rude noises at passers-by.
You look like an angel with your beautiful face
Which God gave you as your saving grace.
Is your world a dream or is it a nightmare?
If only there was a part we could share.
You've shown us affection in your own way.
You've made us laugh and pushed us away.
People stare because they don't know
How hard it is for you to show
Your feelings, except with tears of frustration
Because you lack communication.

They say you're non-verbal, I call you 'non-wordal',
You're noisy, disruptive, you're happy, you're
different.
Richard my brother, I love you a lot.
Trapped in your world that seems so simplistic,
It is a tragedy that you are autistic.

Caroline Allen (11)
Wimbledon High School
London
(Age Category Winner and Highly Commended)
(Roald Dahl Wondercrump School Award)

My school

I like books
and I like toys.
I have friends
and they are boys.

Andrew Robinson (5)
Seven Stars County Primary School
Leyland, Lancs

Start of the day

Silence tiptoes
About the school,
Searching for a noise
To pounce on.
Then a whisper of footsteps
Grows to a roar
As the school bell sounds.
Chairs scrape,
Doors bang,
Pencil tins rattle.
The teacher smacks
A ruler on his desk
Like a pistol shot.
Heads bow to work.
Silence tiptoes
About the school.

Kim Farrell (12)
Debenham High School
Stowmarket, Suffolk

DOODLES IN MY ROUGH BOOK
(poems of school life)

It wasn't me

No one likes me
no one is my friend
no one cares for me
no one plays with me
no one in class likes me
children get me done
for swearing
but I don't
people do things
and they cry
when I touch them
they say don't
and hold their leg
when I really don't kick them
I don't do all the nasty things
they say I do
I'm a good boy really.

Gregory Socas (6)
Haworth First School
West Yorkshire

Bullies

They say things like,
'Shut up!' 'Oi, Smelly!'
'Baby Boy! get out of me way!'
'Gollywog!' 'Fatface!'
They punch, kick, elbow,
push, stare, break your arm
in the middle of the playground
to make you have a nose bleed.
They've got lasers in their eyes,
knives in their teeth,
dangerous music in their brains.
At home, they feel left out
when their mum says
it's time for bed.

Patrick Anderson (7)
Handford Hall County Primary School
Ipswich, Suffolk
(Age Category Winner)
(School of the Year)

My friend

My friend is so special to me.
But sometimes he goes against me.
It is as though
I am the smallest potato
In the plastic bag.

Jackson Ingle (9)
Darell School
Richmond, Surrey

Learning to read

I sat there,
And looked glumly at the page,
My mind aching.
I blinked and the tears came.
The book blurred,
Illegible.
The words slowly melted into little rivers
Running past me,
Tauntingly.
The picture smudged,
Like chalk on a blackboard.
The brown vinyl table,

With fake, black, plastic knots,
Gave demure reflections of my crumpled face.
I blinked the tears away.
And concentrated again.
'H . . . E . . . L . . . L . . . O,' I sounded.
H..E..L..L..O burned in my mind.
H. E. L. L. O. It stirred long dead fires.
H.E.L.L.O. This word,
This word meant so much.
Then, suddenly, 'Hello!' I cried.
And the world replied . . .
'Hello.'

Daniel Ribenfors (13)
Halesworth Middle School
Suffolk
(Age Category Winner)

Giggles

Aggle, waggle,
I write 'a'.

Eggle, weggle,
I write 'e'.

Iggle, wiggle,
I write 'i'.

Oggle, woggle,
I write 'o'.

Uggle, wuggle,
I write 'u'.

Daniel Bishop (6)
Moorings Way Infant School
Southsea, Hampshire

The wrong way round!

I say, I say, I say!
      Something funny happened the other day.
Pavements walked across the people,
And lightning ran away from the steeple,
Walls sunbathed on top of cats
And dogs gave people thousands of pats.
Trees flew from bird-to-bird,
And cats stroked people and those people purred.
Litter threw people into bins
And a house nearby had needles and pins.
People's heads grew out of hair
And someone chased a big black bear.
      One day at school the children tried
      To teach the teacher, and she cried!

Claire Sampson (9)
Friars Grove Junior School
Colchester, Essex

Summertime

Cheers rang out;
We were allowed on the meadow,
First time this year.
We exploded from school
Like racehorses out to grass.
We galloped into the hideouts,
Rediscovering forgotten secrets.
Hidden dens
Were re-vamped
Into this year's mini riding stables.
Free from iron railings and tarmac,
We played
Chain game,
Forty forty,
Kiss, cuddle and torture.
We were one huge family.
The bell clanged for the end of break.
We walked reluctantly
Out of our secret world.
Summer had come again.

Charlotte Castro (14)
Debenham High School
Stowmarket, Suffolk

Language barrier

I blink for an instant
and words become dim,
Furrowed with white lines
the sentences swim.
The back of my eyes
seem to scream with the pain
of a field of barbed letters
attacking my brain,
and shielding the meaning
in symbols and signs,
for the ideas are trapped
behind well-guarded lines,
and against their defences
my willpower is weak.
So I get into bed,
and forget about Greek.

Lucy Howard (15)
Wimbledon High School
London
(Age Category Winner)
(Roald Dahl Wondercrump School Award)

German lessons

Doodles in my rough book,
Daydreams out the window,
How should I spend this German lesson?
Should I bother to answer any questions?

We're going over homework,
No one else has done it,
If they have it's wrong
But I've done it.
I'm a leaf on a deciduous tree in winter,
I bother.

It's easy for me,
Explaining to me
I understand,
As I should,
Being half German,
But when I do, no one else does.

My hand is raised.
Untouched,
I'm abandoned for someone else,
Just like an unwanted child at an orphanage.
They get it wrong, and for the third time,
The teacher explains it incomprehensibly.

Now I am so desperate,
I try to answer every question.
When she complains of the lack of hands,
I shout at her in my mind,
Then why don't you pick me?

She picks someone else,
They get it wrong,
Over and over again.
Is it me
Or is the world repeating itself?
Like the water cycle.

Now I resort to the worst
As she won't pick me,
I push my book with the right answers
In front of my friend's face,
She gets the message
And reads out my answer.
Finally, my wish is fulfilled;
The world stops repeating itself.

Gemma Palmer (13)
Weybridge, Surrey

Wishful thinking

Wind's in the trees,
Frost's in the air.
Geography.
Maps.
The teacher's voice gets hazy,
My world is different;
Sun, sand and the endless lapping
                      of the waves on the shore.
Sipping lemonade and browsing
                         through magazines,
Lying in the sun.
The bell goes.
The map closes.
Next lesson English.
Poetry,
About daydreams;
Now where was I?!

Kate Fellows (11)
St John's C.E. Middle School
Kidderminster

Knock on the door

Knock on the door
and close your eyes
think of a poem that
really rhymes.

Knock on the door
and stamp your feet
think of a song to
clap the beat.

Knock on the door
and nod your head
think of a story
to read in bed.

Knock on the door
and close your eyes
think of a poem
that really rhymes.

Hannah Trembath (7)
Leighfield County Primary School
Uppingham, Rutland

Poem under pressure

I'm trying to write a poem;
The competition rules demand
One more to make up three.
I am a finalist
And my English teacher smiles her pleasure.
The news has spread through the staffroom
Like mould in a bowl of fruit
That cultivates a wonder drug,
As, one by one,
They come to inject me with their enthusiasm,
Infect me with their expectations.
My science teacher
Compares me to a summer's day
As I neutralise some HC1,
And my maths teacher grins
When we pass on the stairs:
'Go for it, Rachel,
Our Poet Laureate soon to be.'
My form tutor requests
A daily progress report –
In confidence, of course –
And the French assistant asks,
At regular intervals,
'Does it go well,
Your wonderful poem?'
Even the headmaster
Crosses his fingers

And raises his eyebrows
In a poem-inspiring way
As I hurry past him.
The library is my only refuge
Where, dodging morale-lifting shouts
And theme suggestions,
I flee to hide among the inanimate books
To create my masterpiece.
It's imperative that I do it now –
After all, I'm excused
My history homework.
The time is right;
But lines and words and time
Won't fit together
And inspiration is fast sinking
In a quicksand of encouragement
My desperate grabs and grasps
Can't penetrate.

At last pen strikes paper
And I write the only thing I can –
'Poem under Pressure'.

Rachel Barrett (16)
Debenham High School
Stowmarket, Suffolk
(Poet of the Year)

Last lesson

I sat on my seat,
My thighs itched,
Stuck to the plastic.
Teacher talked on,
Pointed to a map of Wales.

Outside a bee droned,
In the sky a cloud, 'Africa',
Floated past.
Tennis ball thudded on the court.

The clock on the wall jerked
Out the seconds
In deafening ticks.
Outside, the echo of tennis ball
On racquet.

A dragon fly settled
On the window ledge
Fanning its sparkly, fragile wings.
On the ceiling,
The neon lights flickered.

The boy behind
Kicked my chair,
I ignored him.
The teacher wiped the board

Sending a shower of white chalk dust
everywhere.
A flock of white seagulls
Flew silently past.

The tennis ball popped once more,
3.15 the bell rang.
Commotion,
Rattling of pencil tins,
Fluttering of books,
Clattering of chairs.

The door flung open
We burst out
Into the sunshine,
Scattered like seeds
From a poppy head
Blowing in the wind.

Rosy Pittman (14)
Bishopston Comprehensive
Bishopston, Swansea

Minutes of a Meeting of Words;

Intent: to Form a Poem

1. Present: Forty assorted words:
   Thirteen nouns, commonplace or shocking;
   Eight verbs, sentence-makers, active and busy;
   Nine adjectives, flowery and self-important;
   Six articles, three pairs of twins;
   Three prepositions, shy little words.

2. Apologies for absence: Rhyme refuses to add her chime;
   Reason has left in disgust.

3. Matters arising:
1. The Subject:
   'Russet' proposes Autumn;
   Seconded by Leaves, to meet her own ends.
   Glorious adjectives rush forward,
   Three are suitable.
   Cliché shows its face, sticks out its tongue

Throwing the meeting into pandemonium.
(That was Rhyme –
Where did she come from?)
Subject – school starting?
One for the adjectives
Especially the negatives.

Idea after idea:
   Parody?
   Poems?
   Prose?
   Protection?
   (Rhyme has gone again. Alliteration
   Tired and overworked as usual
   Has done her bit).

Words jostle for position.
PREpositions
are squashed.

There must be something to form a poem about
Poems should be harmonious and moving –
   yet adjectives have gone out of fashion.
They realize it, and retire.
Leaving nouns and verbs to fight it out.
Without a subject, there can be no writing.
               Sun showing
               God dancing
            Bacteria to fight
              Sheep it flies

The meeting has been gatecrashed
The words are at war ...

... suddenly silence.

The poet has fallen asleep.

Gail Trimble (12)
The Lady Eleanor Holles School
Hampton, Middlesex
(*Age Category Winner*)

Fire extinguisher

There's a red fire extinguisher in the corridor.
At night time she comes alive.
She grows stubby legs and wings,
And becomes a red penguin,
Waddling down the corridor,
Peeping in the dark classrooms,
Playing with the computers,
Fiddling till it's time to go.
Contented, she shuffles off,
Back to her high dusty nest.
She waits frozen,
Soon children return to class,
Soon feathers return to tin.

Amy Tullett (10)
Heyworth County Primary School
Haywards Heath, West Sussex
(Age Category Winner)

Busy

Wake up, wake up
Can't
Have to.

Hurry up, hurry up
I am
Quick

There's the bus, there's the bus
Missed it
Have to be faster.

Go on, go on
Bye
Have a nice day.

Don't dream, don't dream
Yes, sir
Work harder.

Eat up, eat up
I am
Come on.

You'll miss the bus, you'll miss the bus
I won't
It's here.

Do your prep, do your prep
Hang on
No.

Bed time, bed time
Haven't finished
Never mind.

Calm down, calm down
Can't
You must

Theo Stocker (11)
Rutland, Leicester

Head Girl

I've never painted a perfect picture
Or written a winning poem.
I've never been good at games
Or chosen for the cross-country team.
I've never been outstanding in any of my lessons
Or had brilliant exam marks.

So why did they choose me?
Have they made a mistake?
Do they think they have picked
The shiniest gem
From the centre of a tray
Of glittering rings?
Can glass glow bright enough?

Katy Styles (15)
Debenham High School
Stowmarket, Suffolk

FORGOTTEN UNDER CHILDHOOD'S TREE
(poems about growing up)

Slowly

Slowly I grow into an old lady.

Slowly a caterpillar changes
into a butterfly.

Slowly the butter melts into
butter sauce.

Slowly the sun sinks and the
moon comes up.

Slowly my sister turns seven.

Slowly I grow bigger.

Slowly it turns to home time.

Victoria Hayman (7)
Heathfield School
Pinner, Middlesex

Growing up

Wow! New bike.
Padded frame, blue and white BMX, my favourite.
'Now don't go on the roads!'
Here I go
Dodge the lamppost, jump a bump,
Around the block 'I'm home!'

Wow! New bike.
Claud Butler, Falcon Warrior, eighteen speed, grip
shift gears, EXCELLENT.
'Remember you haven't got any lights, yet.'
Here I go!
Top gear fifteen, twenty, twenty five miles an hour,
See a boy on a bike like my old one,
'Want a race?'
'Can't. Not allowed on the road.'
Was I really that small?

Dominic Everson (14)
Simon Langton Boys' School
Canterbury

WOW

12 and a half

I am 12 and a half and I'd like to grow some breasts.
I would love to wear a bra because I'm sick of
  wearing vests.

My face is rather spotty, on my hair you could fry an
  egg.
My knees go down to my ankles, why can't I have
  long legs?

I would love to have a boyfriend, someone to call my
  own.
But when I call them up my brace whistles down the
  phone.

I never wear a skirt, I always stick to jeans,
I wouldn't say my legs are hairy but they have to be
  dry-cleaned.

My moods are really weird, sometimes I am the
  perfect child.
And then for no apparent reason I seem to go quite
  wild.

My mum says she can't take no more she's really had her
  lot.
She says I'm either barmy or my hormones have
  gone to pot.

Rebecca Evans (13)
Neverthorpe School
Staveley, Derbyshire

To my first friend

I was a brown-haired Hermia,
And you, Helena, my cherry-twin.
No Athenian grandeur filled our days
But speedwell, sun and trinket toys,
Snow fortresses and paint-blob fields,
And earth-damp grass beneath the mist.
No love juice could make us break friends.

Now we laugh politely at childhood.
Time has ripped apart the cherry stems
And planted us in separate gardens.

Sarah Hunter (14)
Debenham High School
Stowmarket, Suffolk
(Age Category Winner)

The big table

It's been there since I was tiny,
no larger than its leg.
The table in the dining room
where we broke our Sunday bread.
I love that table, so large, so long.
It stood there in the conservatory,
till we had upped and gone.

We took it to our new house,
and ate at it on family occasions,
and it was the sea that we swam in,
the cave we hid from dinosaurs in,
the spaceship that we soared to the moon in.
Through my childhood
it made our house a home.

We moved again, and still it stayed,
this time dismantled in the shed.
It was brought out again for a birthday meal –
it's stayed up till this day.
But it's too big for the house.
Mum and Dad say it's got to go –
come what may.

I love that table, the big table,
the table we swam on,
the cave we hid in,
the spaceship we soared in – my table.

Matthew Facherty (14)
Kidmore End, Oxfordshire

The past, the present, the future

A small child walked
Behind her mother,
Clutching her hand,
Tripping on loose slabs,
Gazing with clear eyes
At her life in front.

An old woman walked
Behind her daughter,
Clutching her hand.
Tripping on loose slabs,
Gazing with cloudy eyes
At little life in front.

Alex Dicker (13)
King Edward's High School for Girls
Birmingham

Comforter

I heard her crying
In her room across the way
And selfishly I wished I hadn't.
I wanted it to stop
And seem as if it never was;
I wanted to sleep untroubled
And wake unknowing.
I didn't want to care.

But, I heard her crying.
It gripped my chest,
It stung my throat
And I remembered all those times
She'd come when I had wept
To sit by me
And tell me stories.

I felt like screaming:
'No, that's not right; you're mistaken.
I cry; you comfort.'
It mustn't change;
We must keep things as they were.

But still her lonely sobbing
Seeped in at my door

And found me
Hiding under my covers.
Silently, I slipped from my bed
And out across the landing
To find her.

Rachel Barrett (16)
Debenham High School
Stowmarket, Suffolk
(Poet of the Year)

Waiting

He sits by the window,
On his seventeenth birthday,
Expecting some cards,
He's waiting, waiting.

He stands on the platform,
At the train station,
Dressed in his khaki,
He's waiting, waiting.

He squats in a trench,
Hears the bombs and the guns,
What are his orders?
He's waiting, waiting.

He struggles in the mud,
Swamped with the dead,
With cuts on his face,
From the barbed wire fence.
The injured cry,
But he can't stop to wait,
While unseen in the dark,
A German gun,
Has him in sight,
A squeeze on the trigger and . . .

He lies on the battlefield,
Motionless and bloody,
Clutching an unmailed letter,
. . . His wait is over.

She sits by the window,
Expecting a letter,
From her soldier in France,
She's waiting, waiting.
Waiting, waiting.

Daniel Lea (12)
Gwersyllt
Wrexham, Clwyd

First impressions

We sit.
You look at me.
I look at you.
Our eyes meet for one split second.
The world stops.
Our gaze ends.
It starts again.
I watch you, as you bury your head in your arms.
Then I look away.
I become aware of you taking a peek at me.
I tell myself I'm imagining things,
No one ever likes me.
Slowly we're less shy.
More relaxed.
Your leg touches mine.
When your hand brushes my arm,
I don't move it away.
The barriers are being broken down.
The gaze lasts longer.
I imagine there's a flame there.
I pray.
I hope.
I want to shout.
I feel like I'm falling in love.
I want to stop it.
I'll only get hurt.
But I'm hypnotised.

I have to walk away.
Cold, I leave.
I want you to follow me.
I'm too shy.
You're too shy.
I've fallen.
It's scary.

Ruth Taylor (16)
Chester, Cheshire
(*Age Category Winner*)

Pretending to myself

I'm going away, but I need to say,
'I'll write.'
Why is that?
The one long summer of jokes and
half-forgotten whispers is over;
Eventually, its memory will merge and
blur like a badly-taken photograph.
I try to reassure myself that
pieces of paper can continue our friendship.
She smiles and hands me her address,
but in her eyes I see the truth:
This part of our life is over,

and soon will be nothing more
than a dog-eared photograph;
Trying to change its future is like
trying to stay a child forever,
As useless as tears,
Or as hopeless as shouting
'I'll write' into an open grave.
Yet, as the coach pulls up in the morning light,
I feel the whole world is leaning forward
and willing me to say
'I'll write.'
I wish I could be honest, and simply say,
'I'd love to write, but time, space and
human nature are dragging me away.'

Nicola Anne Piggott
Wimbledon High School
London
(Roald Dahl Wondercrump School Award)

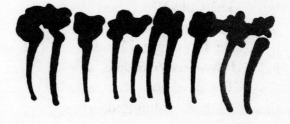

Changing world

The Cold War
Was a war
Of ideologies.
That is what they taught me.
The West,
I was told,
Stood for freedom
And liberty;
While the East
Was a police state,
And freedom
Was restricted.

But now,
The Cold War is over
And the excuses
For hostility and hatred
Have been removed.
The freedom
That was trumpeted
Is being slowly
Eaten away
And eroded
By the people
That we're supposed to trust.

I remember the time
When none of this
Mattered to me;
Where everyone
Who smiled
Was my friend,
And the police were there
To protect,
Not to watch
And follow me.

But maybe I'm paranoid
Maybe I think too much.

The psychiatrist said
That my friend
Thought too much,
That's why she was depressed,
He said.
So he put her on valium
And now
She doesn't think much at all.

Nicholas Bieber (15)
Belsize Park, London

Images

It was an image
Of a younger girl
That you held in your head
As she entered the room.
A child who had smiled,
Held your hand
And found no fault,
Uncritical,
Unquestioning.
A child who had accepted
What you did to her
As something
That was almost love.
That person is now lost
Somewhere beyond
Or just behind your mind.
The corners of your mouth twitched
And your forward-facing eyes
Seemed to stare back
Into your head,
Searching.
Then you frowned
As if you could,
By creasing your brow,
Have somehow channelled the image
Into the room
To come alive

And take her place.
The brutal knowledge
That you forced on her
Has grown to a deeper wisdom
And a new, bruising,
Dark, accusing child
Has replaced the one
That you had nurtured
In your head
And it is an image
That you will never
Have to search for.

Rachel Barrett (16)
Debenham High School
Stowmarket, Suffolk
(*Poet of the Year*)

Sundial

I cannot remember now
Where it is;
The sundial, I mean,
Enclosed by a musty stench, like a wall,
In its bed of decaying fruit.

The sundial was of marble,
The satin of stone,
With faintest engravings
Of princes and thrones –
The orchard its frame.

I cannot remember now
Where it is;
The sundial I mean.
I can only remember
The soft stirring of birds
And the welly-squelch of autumn;
The place is forgotten
Under childhood's tree.

Amanda Rose (15)
Debenham High School
Stowmarket, Suffolk

The end

The moments of silence grow now. Heart-ache
Laughs between us, and as the end nears,
The bridge to you turns brittle: it would break
With my touch, with my love, or with my tears.

My hands which once touched you, tremble. I will say
Nothing, for it would be wrong; wrong to speak.
You have chosen to let go, I can't sway
Your heart, for I am not the love you seek.

Now, there is silence, the distance tugs my heart
And I feel you turn away. The threads wear,
The glass arch shatters, and we fall apart.
I'm bleeding in the splinters of love, and you don't
care.

So forget me, be done with me, let go.
I did love you, did you love me? I don't know.

Christopher Newman (17)
Dunbar, Eastlothian
Scotland

Time

Some may compare you to an old man,
Bent double, bearded white,
Creeping and creaking,
When I was a child you were grey.
All those nights I wished would fly
All those days I prayed would merge.
You never obeyed my childish cries
You were my enemy.

And now as I grow slower you are a child,
Filled with infinite energy.
I want to catch you and tie you down
But you are too fast for me.
And now I regret my calls in the night
My spirit too old to fight.

Abigail Pike (17)
Tunbridge Wells Girls' Grammar School
Kent

The climb

The boy struggles to climb the tree,
Longing for his mother
To give him the last shove.

Depending on one small branch,
He strains
And pulls himself up.
Snap!
The branch can't hold him.
He bumps,
Scrapes
And comes to a thud
On a broad bough.
Shaken, worried, grazed and alone,
He takes one long, deep breath
And then thrusts upwards,
Grabbing any and every branch,
Straining each muscle
And scarring his hands and face.
He is there.
He looks back, down
To the woman,
The one he used to look up to,
And now
There she is . . .
Below him.

Kate Kydd (14)
Debenham High School
Stowmarket, Suffolk

Badlands

Where the horizon is sacred,
because the ground knows its place
and your footsteps last forever
in the murderous sun
a kid in a black car is marking his track
with a shotgun head
loaded with rebellion
he smiles like a film star
and lays another to waste
while his bubble gum girlfriend
drowns in his charm
he's got a haircut and a trigger finger—
and that's all he needs
as he fires his frustrated screenplay
into a bystander's back
but the road that lasts forever
and the misfit, windblown rocks
will remain infinitely longer
than the script written by his gun.

Jamie Huxley (17)
*Bishop Luffa School
Chichester*

THE SOUND OF THEIR VOICES
(poems of other people's lives)

Women bathing

The stillness of waters green
exaggerated by the smooth legato
movements of sensual women.
Rubber ladies sprawled and stretched
with glowing suits of coloured
skin, tight against their arched bodies.

Long flowing locks of hair set free.
The thin white clouds set against
calm, blue skies, gently combed
by the distant house of light.
The soft hand of the sky stroking
the sails of a passing boat
and one jagged rock set apart
from the rest, yet still close.

Sally Talbot (15)
Tunbridge Wells Girls' Grammar School
Kent

Bad football

Bob the wrong keeper,
Sam the own-goal scorer,
John the show-off,
Danny the fouler,
Bill the person that never shoots straight,
Tim the boaster,
(Was that a good goal or what?).
Dean the captain (thinks he's on a ship),
Michael takes free kicks the wrong way
Peter }
Paul } two little dickie birds sitting on the goalposts
Dave trips over fresh air.

Ben Griffiths (10)
Leighfield County Primary
Uppingham, Leics

Breakfast crossword

It depressed him;
It resembled a jail.
There were so many blank white cells
In which the letters,
Recently arrested by the clues at the side,
Could imminently be imprisoned.
Confined to such a small space,
They would surely go mad.
This annoyed him.

He drank his coffee and looked
through the open window,
At the ranges,
Possibilities,
Expanses,
And scopes.
He felt guilty.

He made a decision
To free the letters.
He smiled as he tore the paper,
Annihilating the clues.

Meanwhile the released letters drifted
through the open window,
To the ranges,
Possibilities,
Expanses,
And scopes.

Cheryl Mary Thompson (15)
Teesside High School
Cleveland
(*Age Category Winner*)

The pianist

Slowly, he pulls back the bench.
He sits.
There is a tense pause as the audience is silent.
He brings his fingers to the keys.
Overwhelmingly,
the music floats out
in waves of emotion.
The music is
Strong
Peaceful
Ominous
Delicate
Ever changing . . .
He finishes sensitively,
pausing with fingers still outstretched,
as if playing silence instead of sound.
The audience hesitates again.
The silence is deafening.
One lone pair of hands starts.
The whole concert hall is rocking with applause.
Tears streaming
from her cheeks,
his last notes echoing
in her head,
she runs home
with still the vain hope that . . .
Slowly, she pulls back the bench.

She sits.
She brings her fingers to the keys.
But all
that comes out
is a
Noise.

Mary Jepson (11)
TASIS
Thorpe, Surrey

Softly

Softly the rain drops in the bucket.
Softly the sun rises.
Softly the wars end.
Softly the men drop the guns and be friends.
And softly all the trees grow again.
Softly the men all come,
Home from all over the world.

Ian Holderness (8)
Nienburg School
Germany

In quiet voice

A girl,
Who lives near me,
Who only smiles with fear.
The way she talks,
In quiet voice,
So gentle, hurt, knowing,
And clear,
Suggests to me
That in her life,
She's known a lot of pain,
For when she talks,
In quiet voice,
She sometimes forgets,
And stops,
And starts again.
And sometimes,
When she's talking,
Her voice trails far away.
She says something,
From deep inside her soul,
Then realizes,
Corrects herself,
And continues to say
That everything at home is fine
And she's going to the shops.
But although her voice is happy,
Her eyes are clearly not.

She's holding back her tears inside,
Her voice is a disguise,
A cover up
To hide the fact,
That for her
Life, pain, and misery,
Go hand in hand,
And side
By
Side.

Michelle Small (14)
Ashford, Kent

Miss Rooby's specs

Miss Rooby's specs are small and round,
She bought them new for just one pound,
I was amazed and asked her how.
Surprised, she said, 'I'll tell you now.
The reason why the cost's so low,
Is I got them 40 years ago.'

Annelies Waite (11)
Redland High School for Girls
Bristol, Avon

Feet

A lever to propel the body forward,
A skeleton of many bones
Jointed together.
Tendons, muscles and arch ligaments
Support one another,
A huge machinery of many networks
Delicate but essential.

Miles and miles of terrain to encounter:
The cutting implements of sharp shingle,
The wet feathers of soft sand,
The aromatic needles of stiff pine,
The penance of unforgiving pavements.
The demanding mind offers
No rest, no relief, but
Drives them on, like a machine,
Into the ground.

Katie Hamson (13)
The Lady Eleanor Holles School
Hampton, Middlesex

Rainbow girl

A pile of flowers by the road,
—A cluster of people looking on,
A sunny rainbow in her smile,
My sister crying at a song.

Fragmented life, disrupted norm,
A willing helper in affliction,
The radio's impersonal news
A healing girl's ironic fate.

Seven girls squashed into a pew,
A flower planted in her name,
Nervous words, sympathetic smiles,
But no one asks the question 'Why?'

A fatal secret kept inside,
A cheerful exterior with something to hide,
Although afflicted, shining still:
A light of hope on all our darkness.

Rainbow girl, you will be missed
But your love is with us still
You are sign in the rain
That the sun will come shining through.

*This poem is dedicated to the memory of Karen Broom who
died on the 20th September, 1994*

Helen Chalk (15)
Thorpe St Andrew High School
Norwich

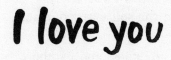

In a boat
they began to
float,
A lady and a
man.
They went
fishing,
For kissing,
Not fish!

Merve Escobado (7)
Southbank International School
London
(Age Category Winner)

Better they didn't know

You sit on the slope with a 'smoke' between your lips,
Blowing through your teeth,
Without taking the cigarette from your mouth.
With narrowed eyes you study the map,
And you trace your finger along the route,
The route you were to follow,
The route you didn't take.
You look up, spit out the cigarette,
And grind it into the soil with your heel.

All around you, greenness and bamboo,
Enveloping you, strange noises,
Drowning you out, the jungle,
Alive,
Waiting –
And you cough loudly,
Then realize where you are,
And hold back the next cough,
Until your throat itches.

Then you get to your feet,
Folding the map into a tight square and
Stuffing it into your helmet.
The men, seeing you rise,
Do the same, like sheep in a field.

You hear the canteens being closed and
screwed up tight,
And the groaning of new boots in action.

You haven't told the boys yet,
About the route you were to follow,
The route you didn't take,
Some of them so young,
And naive,
Better they didn't know,
You thought,
Better they didn't know.

So you smile artificially,
Being kinder than usual
And they sense this.
You were never good at pretending.
'You OK Captain?' they ask,
'Sure,' you answer, 'Sure.'
So they leave you alone,
And you continue your trek, you, and the men,
Trying to find the landing zone
That you won't ever see.

'Missing in Action,' they'll say,
Back home,
'Missing in Action, in Vietnam.'
And your mother will cry

For a son who went astray,
From the route you were to follow,
The route you didn't take.

Will you still,
After days of walking in a circle,
Remain silent,
Repeating to yourself,
Better they didn't know,
Better they didn't know,
Until the jungle,
Alive,
Waiting –
Swallows you up, you, and the men,
Until the jungle swallows you up?

Zoe Layton (13)
St Nicholas' School
Harlow, Essex
(Age Category Winner)

With pained delight

Dark room glows
With pained delight.
Nice day fades
To soulful fight.

Rope hangs down
Watch him now
Strange-shaped loop
He'll take a bow.

His muscles now
Tensioned, tight,
He takes a step
With pained delight

Downward falling,
Breathing's slight,
Breaking free
With pained delight.

Michael Molloy (15)
St Michael's Senior High
Lurgan, Co. Armargh
Northern Ireland

Despair

She was lonely
She was sad,
She walked the streets
She wasn't bad.

What had she done.
To come to this?
No roof tonight
So much to miss.

The cardboard box
So grim and cold,
No running water
No sheets to fold.

To benefit office
The daily rush,
For endless hours
The queues that push.

She walks the streets
So short of food,
Her head hung low
in blackest mood.

Her family gone
in such despair,
Life is over—
But who's to care?

Louise Doyle (13)
Fairbourne, Gwynedd

Old age

My skin gets wrinkles.
I try to run,
I can't I can't run.
I need a rest.
My body bends over slightly.
I need a walking stick,
I need a rest.
I need a rest.
I sit down on my chair and relax.
Keeping warm by the fire.
Getting older and older every day.
I need a rest.
I need a rest.

Bryony Wilmott (6)
Binfield C of E Primary School
Bracknell, Berkshire

Traffic lights

Middle-aged man
In smoke-filled car,
Dreaming of evenings
In beer-soaked bar,
And watching the rain
Splash on to the glass,
He watches and waits,
As the other cars pass.
The traffic lights change
From green through to red,
And he hums as he sorts
Through the thoughts in his head.
He drives past the station,
Now silent and bare,
And the streetlights flash on,
Though there's nobody there.
Turning the corner,
He pulls up the drive,
His wife has been waiting
For him to arrive.
She does the washing,
He watches TV,
And they talk of the things
That they wanted to be,
And later on,
As she turns out the light,
And the sound of their voices

Melts into the night,
They see their ambitions
Falling to dust,
Suburban dreams,
Starting to rust.

Louise Richardson (14)
Durrington High School
Worthing, Surrey

Homeless

I stand on the stage;
Our Christmas pantomime
Is 'Hansel and Gretel'.
She stands on the dry earth,
In her hand
The tattered remains of a book.
Is it Hansel and Gretel?

I stand in the spotlight,
In an ocean-blue frock
And starched white apron.
She stands in the scorching sun
In a shabby grey dress, limp
And three sizes too big.

I stand as Gretel,
Shut out from my home
And pretending to shiver.
She stands in the desert,
Locked out from her village,
Wishing for a home.
She has no trail
Of stones or breadcrumbs,
No gingerbread house.

Leila Anani (13)
Debenham High School
Stowmarket, Suffolk
(Age Category Winner)

The Ford Fiesta
(*After 'Tyger, Tyger' by William Blake*)

Ford Fiesta! shining bright
In the roadworks of the night
What poor mortal's hand can feel
The plastic texture of thy wheel?

In what distant little town
Shone the roofrack of thy crown?
On what wheels dare he aspire?
What the hand dare seize the tyre?

And what craft, and O! what skill
Could thy engine tank to fill?
And when the engine 'gan to start,
What dread spanner? What dread art?

What the hammer? What the deal?
In what furnace was thy steel?
What the worker? Whose dread touch
Dared make thy deadly engine clutch?

When the Belisha beacons glow'd,
And all the flowing traffic slow'd,
Did he smile his work to see?
And are you kin to Model T?

Ford Fiesta! shining bright
In the roadworks of the night
What poor mortal's hand can feel
The plastic texture of thy wheel?

Bridget Rose Collins (13)
Tunbridge Wells Girls' Grammar School
Kent

War

Crashing
Roaring
Conflict
Despair
Fighter planes threatening in the air.

Blasts
Explosions
Terror
Fright
Air-raid shelters, a home for the night.

Scream
Shriek
Ache
Weep
Sodden trenches deep and bleak.

Bold
Young
Slaying
Crying
Uniformed soldiers young and dying.

Fatherless
Motherless
Hungry
No home
Isolated orphans sad and alone.

Destruction
Hatred
Darkness
Pain
Bloody wars – all in vain.

David Leslie (10)
Llanidloes C.P. School
Llanidloes, Powys

Strawberry fields remembered

'Aye, they were strawberry fields,'
he used to say,
'None of them little boxes when we came.'
And then he'd wave his hand, with great disdain,
Over the strawberry fields which now remain;
For these are all the modern kind –
Suburban supermarket kind,
The plastic-packed synthetic kind,
As tasteless as their name;
For nothing ever stays the same.

That garden was his life,
he used to say,
And strawberries would one day bring him fame;
So on his hillside lawn he'd dream till late,
A manor lord surveying his estate.
He always grew the proper kind –
The real old-fashioned country kind,
Mouth-melting luscious juicy kind,
World champions, he'd claim –
But nothing ever stays the same.

His home was by the fire,
he used to say,
His favourite chair beside the glowing flame.
I used to play him all his favourite tunes
On home-made jam and muffin afternoons;
He always loved the Scottish kind,
The banks-and-braes and bonny kind,
The singing-with-your-mouth-full kind.
We loved him. It's a shame
That nothing ever stays the same.

Gemma Louise Burford (17)
Old Bursledon, Hampshire

Peace under an English heaven

Every week we trudge by.
Our blazers flapping in the sea breeze,
Ties askew,
—Quiet murmurs of respect as our
Grey dress reflects your tombstone.
Each Sunday, when the bells
Draw me near, I appear on the
Gravel path and stare:
You are a distant name, so lovingly
Engraved.
But now the lichen grows on your southerly
Face.
The cream of the nation they say – I don't
Doubt it;
But what of themselves, what
Of me
As we stare at you,
Just names on the plaques,
Faces on the shelves?
Yet you smile, content despite the
Lead lodged firmly in the chambers
Of your silenced heart.
May you rest in peace.

Ian Napier (13)
Beeston Hall School
Norfolk

Under the pier

The tide's out,
But the old fisherman's in.
Standing there staring with rocky eyes,
He's transparent,
Like a jelly fish breathing in a watery breeze,
He does not move,
His hair like the nets he once knew,
His nose an old seafishing weight,
No mouth,
But teeth, teeth like steel bolts.
His body, a deck polished and shiny,
Legs, the masts of a ship,
With two turned-over crows' nests for feet,
Suddenly, the fisherman fades,
Then gone,
The tide's back in,
The fisherman back out;
Sitting on the curve of the sea,
He waits for his next catch.

Craig Stammers (13)
Halesworth Middle School
Suffolk

I'll be there on Friday

Dear Mick
  I hope you got over that bug you had. I tried to phone
you but no one was home so I thought I'd write you a note.
It is with deep regret that we announce
  This is pretty rare actually – me having time to write
a letter on a Monday morning.
  the death of
  Michael Gordon Murray
I'm going to be over your way on Friday, so I thought
maybe we could meet up for a coffee or something.
  who passed away peacefully in his sleep
How long has it been now? Must be almost a year since
we got together.
  after a short illness
We really must meet up more often!
  on Monday 7th February
How is Jane these days? And Sarah, and little Tim?
Why, he must be almost ten now.
  deeply mourned by his wife Jane and children, Sarah
  and Timothy.
As I say, I'll be round your way on Friday. We could
meet up.
  The funeral will be held at
Shall we say by St Mary's?
  St Mary's Church, Smitham

I'll be there at 11.00, unless you call to say you can't make it.

on Friday 11th February at 11.00 am.
See you there.
Yours ever,
Alan.

Anna Sargeant (16)
Wimbledon High School
London
(Roald Dahl Wondercrump School Award)

Old people

Old people
They're crinkly
And they're grey
And they're happy all day!

Emily-Jane Wilkinson (7)
Moorings Way Infant School
Southsea, Hampshire

WONDERCRUMP POETRY!   153

The Visit

Sinking into old woven chairs,
Bodies sucked into the fabrics,
The heavy, prominent smell,
Of decay and artificial heat.
Some swing their heads on scrawny necks,
Releasing a weird alienated cry,
Dribble gliding from their puckered opening.
Others sit and gaze deafly,
Their eyes screened with a clear enamel,
Resting on single still objects.
Their skin is creased and well worn,
Faded to a deathly shade of grey.
Fingers, columns of crooked bone,
Screwed into a ball of compressed skin.
Parched hair could easily be separated
Strand by strand,
Not grey, not white, but the remainder
Of a once strong and vibrant colour,
Now scraped through to the core.
Their obsolete clothing
Embraces the skeleton beneath.
Around them a scattering of photographs
Smiling faces of loved ones,
Now unknown.

Caroline Newton (15)
Bishop Luffa School
Chichester, West Sussex

THEY MUNCHED AND THEY CRUNCHED

(stories of the animal world)

In the water

In the water is a water snail
Slithering along,
Singing a song . . .
And gone.

On the water
Is a water skater.
It skates so fast
That the others are last.

Rhys Grant (6)
Combs Ford County Primary School,
Stowmarket, Suffolk

Fishing

I looked at my face in the water
and I watched the fish in the bucket.
They swam in a daze,
touching their soft lips on the side, gently,
and wondered at their prison.
Their lips stuck to the sides like suction pads

and pulled away like plungers.
One of them swam to the top
and showed me his lips.
He was a silver roach
and he glittered like quartz.
He opened his mouth for air
and inside was a black manhole, but not as big.
He made a frantic dash for the bottom
and swam around and around . . .
the wall of death at a motor bike show.
He caused a whirlpool
and then he stopped.
I had had enough.
I tipped them back, gently, into the water.

A little water snail crawled up the side of the bucket.
I flicked him back, filled it with water . . .
and watched.

Jonathan Leech (12)
Halesworth Middle School
Suffolk

The otter

I search the lagoon
And see two black pebbles,
Glittering with watery sunshine.
The earth around them
Is rich and dark.
The sudden movement
Of a fish,
A carefully moulded spearhead,
Draws you from your trance.
The pebbles light up;
The earth crumbles
Into tiny strands.
Your Brylcreem coat,
Carefully styled by your mother,
Rises to the surface
In a wild ambush.
   You are such a bully!
Picking on the small and weak.
Fish part
Like curtains
Drawn by your fat fingers.
Graceful, underwater ice dancer,
You shoot off,
Then slip on to the bank.
Your too-short trousers
And sweat-drenched jersey,
Now blemished by mud.

How your mother will scold!
For your well-slicked hair
Now stands on end
Above your cheeky face,
Searching for more mischief.

Eleanor Borer (12)
Halesworth Middle School
Suffolk
(*Age Category Winner*)

My pet alligator

He crawls through the rooms
He likes to watch TV
And he almost eats everything
If he can
But if he doesn't like the food
He gets very mad
So we give him food he likes
Just to be on
The safe
side.

Thomas Bull (6)
St Bede's Prep School
Eastbourne, East Sussex

The crab

There you lie,
Buried in sand.
An armoured vehicle,
In your desert camouflage.
You move stealthily,
Like a tank,
Sideways.
Your tubular eyes,
With the black round ends,
Are little black pin heads.
You are the ballroom dancer,
Who has lost his partner,
And can only dance
The side step shuffle.
But you are the champion boxer,
The aggressive fighter,
With huge outstretched gloves.
And when you lose,
You scuttle off,
Under a rock . . .
And then you are a scared child,
Hiding from your parents.
As you sink back

Into the sand,
There you lie,
An armoured vehicle,
In your desert camouflage.

Gordon Cullingford (11)
Halesworth Middle School
Suffolk

Beetle

Beautiful black beetle
with six strong legs
looking for a home
to lay her eggs.

She looks all round
to find a spot
that's not too cold
and not too hot.

She finds the perfect,
peaceful home
underneath a damp, dark stone.

James Rowley (9)
Threshfield School
Threshfield, Nr Skipton

The bat

The bat is . . .
Scrumpled-up brown fabric,
With bin liner wings.
Swooping swiftly, but silently
Through the dark forbidding trees.
The bat is the highwayman of the forest.
Insects avoid him,
But he is so silent
They don't hear him.
They are shocked silly,
Dancing about
From toadstool to treetop.
'Hands up!' the highwayman squeaks
Before he gobbles them up.
But the bat is also . . .
The ugly sister at the ball,
Turned aside,
Cursed by all.
He flies once more,
Flitting daintily,
A mouse,
With razor-sharp teeth.
Nimbly dodging the trees,
His glossy black eyes
Glisten in the moonlight,
Like cats' eyes in the road.
His claws are . . .

The highwayman's pistols,
But grey and worn,
The colour of seal pups' skin
And winter mornings.
His radar sense in the pitch darkness
Guides the highwayman back to his lair,
Where he hangs,
Oblivious to the world,
Asleep.

Rachael Charlotte Minton (12)
Halesworth Middle School
Suffolk

No rat

Squeaky rat
Purring cat
Cat and rat
Fat cat
No rat

Alexander Denton (7)
Haworth First School
West Yorkshire

The butterfly

The butterfly is an old lady's ballgown.
Motheaten with age,
The colours have faded but are still startling.
The wings are as fragile as rice paper . . .
One false move and they will rip.
It flies up to the sunlight
Where the tissue paper wings glisten,
Like the glazed eyes of her porcelain dolls.
Perfect in every part,
It flutters.
Each movement is reflected in the old lady's eyelids,
Always twitching,
Even when they are closed.
Its body is a tiny silk muff,
Just as sacred, just as silky,
Only shrunk seven times.
It flies out of a window
Into a spider's web,
Where its life leaves it.
Out of fashion, out of style,
Like the ballgown.

Jennifer Wagg (12)
Halesworth Middle School
Suffolk

Snails

Snails are squidgy and squashy,
Their shells are shiny,
They stick on the wall.
They slide down once again.
So they squidge squodge down the lane.
As they walk, they eat lots of leaves and
maybe some trees.
They are very annoying.
What makes them so?

Hungry they munch and they crunch.
The snails are so slippery.
They ruin your plants and trees,
They ruin your trees and leaves.
But when they get babies, it's worse
They go everywhere.
They ruin every garden.
They are quite a nuisance eating that grass.
When they finish they go
Berp!

Christopher Watters (7)
Greasby Infants
Wirral

Rosie super rabbit

Rosie my rabbit is super big.
She can run as fast as a jet
And as fast as Concorde.
Her teeth are long and yellow like knives.
She has two at the top and two at the bottom
And her whiskers are like spikey icicles.
Her ears stick up like two fingers.
They have got veins.
They are pink – like lipstick
And so are her eyes.
She has got a sniffy nose.
Her fur is as white and soft as the middle bit of bread
(except for the dirty bits on the bottom of her feet).
She crunches up dandelion leaves
And sometimes she can fly
(but don't tell anyone).
She lies down on my legs
But she scratches me sometimes.

Alex Coburn (4)
Berwick Upon Tweed
Northumberland

Spiders

Their movement is strangely mechanical,
Scuttling about their unknown business,
They seem ashamed, the way they hide.
I found one once in the bathroom,
Squeezed against the shiny, white wall,
Pretending it wasn't there.
We think they come from the attic.
But they are elusive
Appearing and disappearing
Like morning dewdrops,
Like clouds on a windy day.
They look old
Like something locked in the dark for a long, long
time.
A dusty brown-black,
Their legs are dry twigs
Brittle and fragile.

Emma Lewis (11)
Oxford High School
Oxford

Friends of the sea

Soft,
Silky
Skin.
Matted
Baby
Fur.
Black,
Grey,
White,
Brown.
Common,
Rare,
Common,
Rare.
Fur,
Gun,
Fur,
Gun,
Bang,
Dead!
Bang,
Dead!
No more left,
All gone,
Goodbye.

Sell the fur,
Sell the skin,
Make a coat,
Gloves to put my hands in.
The friends are dead.
The friends are dead.
All gone,
Goodbye.
They are all gone,
They are all dead,
There are none left.
Murdered by the hunter.
I want to see one,
Want to care.
But the seals are gone,
Gone,
Gone.
The seals have gone
Forever.

Save the seals,
Or say
Goodbye.

Zena Bradbeer (11)
Abbotswood Junior School
Yate, Bristol

Guinea pigs

(Benji bought his guinea pigs from Pet Pals up the road from his house. Benji's mum and dad had planted a new garden. The guinea pigs ate the plants. They, in turn, were nearly eaten by a fox that ran along the back of the garden wall).

Very cold
Nearly froze.

Ran away
Nearly lost.

Tried to climb
Nearly dropped.

Saw a fox
Nearly caught.

Ate the garden
Nearly sold.

Lola wants them
Lola nearly got them.

Benji Inwood (6)
Darell School
Richmond, Surrey
(Age Category Winner)

Cow

Hot chocolate eyes
Stared down at me,
Resentfully,
As though it was a crime to pick mushrooms.
Another pair . . .
And another . . .
And even more.
They surrounded me,
With their fixed glare,
As though trying to push me into the ground.
Running would be no good,
Cornered by a mass of warm fans,
Gently ruffling my hair.
Udders swung,
As they stared long and hard,
Steadily chewing cud.
Long strings of spit-like bungee ropes descended
From their rubbery lips.
Steam rose from their nostrils
And drifted through the air,
Like mist from the sea.
Then, turning, the cows plodded slowly off
Through the grass.
And left me to pick my mushrooms.

Dulcie Titchiner (13)
Halesworth Middle School
Suffolk

The stick insect

The stick insect is a delicate grass sculpture,
a wobbling tent frame.
She looks so innocent from far away,
but when you get close, she's fearsome.
Her eyes are mean, a dot of paint, tiger's eyes.
Her jaws are curved, vicious,
but she eats only privet.
Her body is covered with stubble, an unshaven face.
She doesn't move often,
but when she does, she moves like an angry boxer,
elbows out, fists forward.
Her skin is like a wrinkled sweet paper,
in segments, like a stack of paper cups.
Knock her leg, and she rears up one side,
squatting, her leg raised in self defence.
She doesn't know you're not going to hurt her.

Andrew Duff (13)
Halesworth Middle School
Suffolk

Rabbit on the road

It wasn't us; we didn't do it.
But we stopped.
It was writhing, convulsive,
Like a heart pulsating.
It tried to run, to keep going
But its legs
Were covered in red, like treacle.

'Kill it!'
A moth flew
As the Doc-Martened mercy-bringer
Stomped towards it.
I couldn't look.

Before he got back into the car
He wiped his boots.

Sarah Farthing (15)
Debenham High School
Stowmarket, Suffolk
(Age Category Winner)

Omega

The white horses stand,
Heads into the sharp night gusts;
Their manes and tails fight
And lash in the violent squall.
Their pricked ears
Are fixed on something
Beyond their tidal boundaries
That makes their great bellow-lungs
Rattle and snort.
Through the roaring blast and blow
And the shrill moan of the land fillies,
They sense the coming of something
Beyond even their noble comprehension,
Something that will choke and strangle
With such deadly silence.

The great white horses stand
In their awe-inspiring ranks,
Their rolling flanks quivering
In anticipation of the inevitable
Destruction of their blue-green aqueous pastures.

Rachel Barrett (16)
Debenham High School
Stowmarket, Suffolk
(Poet of the Year)

Circus

The audience roars; the poodles are on.
They hop and they jump
And then leap through a hoop.
The girl with the horses
Is riding bareback.
The horses are gleaming
With feathers and jewels;
Cameras are flashing
To capture the fun,
While down in the dank, cold,
Windowless cellar,
The elephants, lions, tigers and camels
Are waiting their turn in the ring.
The oldest performer,
Chim-chim, the elephant,
Rocks backwards and forwards
In her tiny cell.
Her chain-grey skin
Is tarnished baggy and lined;
Her oyster-shell toenails
Are scuffing the floor.
The door bursts open;
The trainer appears
And leads Chim-chim away.
The mildew smell of the dingy marquee
Reminds Chim-chim of home
And the Indian sun.

Her trainer pulls her accordion trunk,
A signal for Chim-chim to jump
Up on to the tub
That is plainly too small.
She clumsily hops
Like a fat ballerina
But her old ankles slip
On the slug-skin floor.
What use is a slow, old,
clumsy elephant?
Her time at the circus
Has come to an end.
There will be no funeral bell;
Only more space in the cellar.

Emily Sands (14)
Debenham High School
Stowmarket, Suffolk

My cocker spaniel
(Bonnie)

I'm admired for my ears. Three cheers.
I'm admired for my paws. Applause.
And if somebody chased the cat,
And if somebody chewed the mat,
And if somebody jumped the wall,
And punctured next-door neighbour's ball,
It wasn't me.

I'm admired for my eyes, surprise.
I'm admired for my smile, worthwhile.
And if somebody went upstairs,
And covered beds in doggy hairs,
And if somebody climbed a seat,
And left the marks of muddy feet,
It wasn't me.

Joanne Brown (12)
Thorpe St Andrew High School
Norwich

Fox

Foxes are unique
my mum just won't
believe me. She says
they are horrid
creatures.
I dream of them
sly and sleek.
Only chickens would
agree with my mum.

Louisa Keylock (9)
St Andrew's County Primary
North Lopham
Norfolk

Scary

I saw a dragon.
The dragon was hairy.
He ate lots of children.
He was very scary.

Lorna Mann (5)
Littlefield School
Liphook, Hampshire

The giraffe

Long-necked gentle creature
Why are your soft brown eyes so sad?
Do your winged ears
Sense the changing times?

Long-necked gentle creature
Will your neck go on growing forever?
Can we trace the roads of Africa
On your smooth brown skin?

Long-necked gentle creature
Your symmetry lies upon you
Like a jigsaw puzzle
Can we ever find the missing piece?

Long-necked gentle creature
With your swift and graceful run
Can you escape from the future
And remain untouched by man?

Charlotte Last (11)
Stamford High School
Lincs

Dragon

At the bottom of our garden
beside the shed, in amongst
the ivy and conifers,
living in a paint tin with
piles of breeze blocks around it
I found a dragon. Its nest
was made from gone-off fireworks,
old roof tiles and compost.
I saw her every day
at the crack of dawn.
I fed her on old oil cans,
petrol, tyres, curry, capsicums,
fried chips and neutron stars.
One Wednesday I found she'd gone
leaving behind thousands of
three-toed footprints
and a lump of neutron star.

Ashley Wallington-Owens (9)
Handford Hall County Primary School
Ipswich, Suffolk
(School of the Year)

Rabbit's skull

The skull,
layered,
like papier mâché,
lace covered,
like bleached fishbones,

fragile,
but in one piece,
cracks like shattered glass,
edges like rough fossils,
jaws chattering to open.

In my imagination
it dares to look,
gleams in my eye,
and winks.

Clare Woolston (13)
Halesworth Middle School
Suffolk

THE SUN IS A CUPCAKE

(poems of the natural world)

Just wood

I'm crucified to a spot,
In some forgotten piece of land.
A carrot for me sniffer,
A stick for me 'and.

Staked through me back
And some nails in me arms,
Oh yes, I'm a saviour
Not told of in silly yarns.

The stillness of the dark,
When all is sharp and clear,
Is when I'm unemployed;
A cross causes no fear.

Listening to the night lark,
Or the moody moan of the cattle,
Does nowt to hide the boredom,
Of waiting for the battle.

But the night and gloom cracks,
And sunlight seeps on through,
An' I'll bellow and wave me arms,
To save those seeds for you.

But do I get any thanks,
For keepin' you all fed?
'That uns goin' all rotten!'
That's what the farmer said.

So I'm just doin' me duty,
An' fendin' off them crows,
An' wavin' me heavy arms,
Defendin' all his rows:

When 'im who put me up 'ere,
Comes down and in cold blood
Hacks me to small pieces,
And turns me into wood.

Gareth Goodall (16)
Thomas Alleyne's High School
Uttoxter, Staffs

Forest

Here a worm of light
wriggles through the trees,
the only sound is
the crunch of leaves.
Here twigs tug your hair,
mud sucks at your boots.
Here fur is caught on barbed wire,
centipedes and woodlice chew bark,
a circle of flattened bluebells
and cracked snail shells
where something has slept.
Here poorman's beefsteak
bulges from an oak,
clingfilm suffocates a wood pigeon.
Here ashes scatter across
the forest floor, and
trees scream out under the axe.

Daniel James (9)
Handford Hall County Primary School
Ipswich, Suffolk
(School of the Year)

Wood

Sawn stumps – ivy clad, bare-ended, sleeping;
Rotten bark stays still, with wood-lice crawling;
Brushwood, prickly, waiting for the unwary;
Wood chips, crunchy noises as you step.
Shavings and dust between the lifeless stalks;
Wood logs mark paths between the hazel stems.
Logs, evenly cut, are splinter-free;
Wooden poles, freshly sawn and smelling of creosote.

Newly cut branches, piles of wood,
Tiny sticks show where the tree once stood.

Daniel Yarnton (9)
Combs Ford County Primary School
Stowmarket, Suffolk

Sunset

Magical Sunset
Over the silent forest
Lullaby sweet song

Alexa El-Kayem (6)
Southbank International School
London

Bright sun

The sun blusters
with golden shine.
You wear a bikini
and sunglasses
and the swimming pool
is bright blue.
The flowers burst out
in beautiful colours
and the trees, the leaves
are brown and green
and red.

Laura Evers (5)
Upper Wortley Primary School
Leeds

The rain drop

A big rain drop falls
More come down to play with Earth
Rainbow colours rise.

Scott Diamond (6)
Southbank International School
London

Umbrellas

Oil-slicked with rain, dripping, splashing,
Tight cotton stretched taut over wooden ribs.
Upturned boats, floating, gliding,
Overlapping wings in the pastel sky.

Sun reflecting from soaked hats, glistening,
shimmering,
Grey-blue blanket, sheltering a sodden clan.
Sun-bathed tortoise, drying, basking,
Dull flamingoes perched on one delicate leg.

Suddenly, faces, of man, woman, child.
The boats collapse,
                    the bird settles,
                                    the blanket is folded.

The sun evaporates the drops, sparkling, glimmering.
A small girl shatters her quivering reflection.
The land starts to recover, drenched, drowned,
Umbrellas are hung over one's arm once more.

Hannah Peggs (15)
Tunbridge Wells Girls' Grammar School
Kent

The geranium

Scarlet red petals and emerald green leaves,
Stand to attention,
On their long thin stems,
Defending their window sill,
Like brave soldiers in their red coats,
Day and night,
Brightening up every corner of the room.

Sian Watson (11)
Crossways Junior School
Thornbury, Bristol

Clouds

The breeze sweeps them along
Across the broad blue sky, like sheep,
They gather at the grey mountains
They cluster together.

Martin Witty (8)
St Keverne County Primary School
Cornwall

Autumn

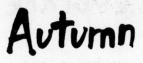

Little shuffles of fallen leaves –
clumps of hair from balding trees.
Syrupy dollops of sunlight
plopping into puddles,
and the ground draining Summer away.

Fields dripping with corn –
God's hot-buttered toast.
Gathering words in the woods,
and being hijacked by
mini hedgehog burs.

Sycamore seeds, giggling,
like windmilling children;
The bonfire choirs,
and the wind reading bedtime
stories to the late light.

Sarah Stringer (15)
St Bede's School
Redhill, Surrey
(*Age Category Winner*)

The sun is a cupcake......

The sun is a cupcake, with yellow icing,
Rays of bright light float off it
like powdered sugar.
It is as hot as fire,
As it sits in its own oven,
Slowly baking so it is crisp to the touch.
Gradually the sun gets lower and lower,
Until it is only half visible.
Someone has taken a huge bite out
of the cupcake.
The night is having a midnight feast.

Catherine Garnett (11)
Notting Hill and Ealing High School
London

My apple

My apple is juicy, round and red,
It grows up high above my head.
My apple is a sphere just like the earth,
I measured my apple around the girth.
My apple's shiny as if polished with pledge,
My favourite fruit, I tasted a wedge.
My apple was tangy, crunchy and sweet,
Ripe and plump and ready to eat.
It's gone brown now it's getting old,
Parts of it are covered in mould.
Leaking juice like sticky oil,
It's rotting down now to feed the soil.

Daniel Walmsley (9)
Roecliffe CT School
Boroughbridge, York

Winter views

(Much ado at the mortuary)

The view from my bedroom window is like the
surface of the moon,
cold and bleak, but impossibly beautiful.
Even though the cold wind blows, tossing the tree
around like an innocent and overwhelmed lover
caught up in a Shakespearean plot,
the garden is as serene as the face of the sleeping.

Looking out, I suddenly start to walk along
the cold blank walls of the mortuary,
scrupulously sterilized to burn away life's residue.
Thanks to a wipe and a scrub
you would never guess what happens here,
what creepy goings on occur within these walls.
The silver scalpels though give the game away,
rows and rows of them like teeth beaming falsely.

The mortuary of the garden,
that terrible but intriguing winter death camp
is as cold as the blood of a snake.
The corpses of trees, flowers, plants, stand around,
frozen lifeless,
as straight as doors and coming up to a crisp.
These dead bodies look astoundingly calm,
not surprised at all to have died,

for Death came, expected and ultimately accepted.
How beautiful they all look now, empty and serene
as female spirits
they stand, crackling like burnt hair, apart from
everything.
And yet, they appear to be thinking almost,
paused in contemplation and inner thoughts:
haughty saints and coma victims they remind me of.

The garden is Siberia,
devoid of anything I would want and desperately cold.
The ground is as dead, as dead as the tree,
and the face of every past relic stares out blankly, like
mummies
or macabre dolls hidden in the lofty, spider-webbed
attic
Beady plastic eyes that watch you, dead calm
But look as if they could come to life
at any given moment.

Duncan Lindan Chappell (16)
Broadstairs, Kent

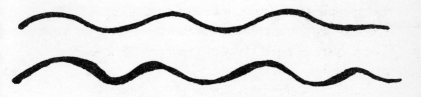

Lullaby

(Barney's little sister has a mobile above her cot. It has stars and a moon with a face on the moon.)

The stars are blazing,
The moon's overhead,
The world all around us
Is going to bed.

Down in the alley
The darkness is deep,
The man in the moon
Is falling asleep.

Barney Waite (age 10)
Darell School,
Richmond, Surrey
(Age Category Winner)

The Autumn Poem

Autumn is a lion
Whose roar blows the leaves off the trees.
It tramples down ripe corn,
Scares the birds to the south,
And eats the sun up.

James Paul Myers (11)
Stowmarket, Suffolk

Sunset

Going through the day 'til half past three.
When the sun's gazing down hills,
Sun shrinking softly, slowly shining,
Soaking in the ground.
As the sun's making progress going down,
And the sun makes fire to crack glass,
Rippling reflections in the water and fire in it too,
and a night falls.

Robert Smith (7)
St Margaret's School
Angmering, West Sussex

Letters of the cave

Long before man heard the metronome of time
And stole it for his own creation,
Hunting it with baying bells
And snipping with the clinical arms of clocks,
I neighboured with the sea.
Well I knew the tang of salt and spray
And the alphabets of wave and tide,
Forming poems in the sands each day.
The sweep of words and swell of tide
Lyrics to creation's theme
Harmonised by stars and sky,
Sighed through underwater forests green.

Then man emerged through leaf and fern;
He danced our strains and stamped our tunes,
Mind-netting our unfolding songs
And trapping them in my sides in runes.
Still inside the strokes of jagged straights
The flowing message captive waits
For forming of the final words
At last, at the reining of time.

Efchi Michalacopoulos (16)
Putney, London
(*Age Category Winner*)

Beyond the trees

Beyond the trees in the far, far distance,
There's a log cabin,
And a woodpecker up in a tree.

Beyond the trees in the far, far distance,
There's a brook of crystal clear water,
And a deer drinking nearby.

Beyond the trees in the far, far distance,
There's a bog of croaking frogs,
And a puddle of water.

Beyond the trees in the far, far distance,
There's a blue jay
Making its nest.

Beyond the trees in the far, far distance,
There is something I cannot quite see.
Could it be?
The log cabin
The woodpecker
The brook of clear water
The deer drinking nearby
The blue jay and its nest, or
The bog of croaking frogs.

I wonder which one it is.
Maybe they aren't there anymore.
Maybe they're gone.

Beyond the emptiness in the far, far distance,
There aren't any trees to be seen,
What has happened?
Where have the trees gone?

Beyond the emptiness in the far, far distance,
There aren't any flowers,
There isn't any grass.

Beyond the trees in the far, far distance,
Has always been a special place to me,
So don't destroy that special place,
Beyond the trees in the far, far distance.

Martin Cheffins (11)
TASIS
Thorpe, Surrey

Water

Water is warm, refreshing, crystal clear,
cold like ice-cream, hot for a bath,
speeding down waterfalls,
salty in the sea. Water
could be spraying everyone in the face.
It could be dirty, or clean, pure.
You could be crying, with tears
running down your face.
It could be creeping up flannels.
It could be used in a foot spa.
It could be leaking from a tap;
drip, drip, drip, drip.

James Richards (6)
Sacred Heart RC Primary School
Hastings, East Sussex.

A spell to take away the badness from the world

Drain the milk from a dandelion
The wings of a jet
The sap from a bee
Take a fin from a sea maiden
Stir the light from a star
Sift the foam from the sea
Roll the colours from the rainbow
Take away the red from the rose
Mix the fire from the sticks of hell
Slice the sting from the nettle
Take away the dark from the sky
Take the light from God
Mix with all God's power
Puff
All the badness goes.

Peter Fitton and Kevin Horton (8)
Castleton County Primary School
North Yorkshire

Calling

The sky is grey,
And snow is falling.
The winter winds are
        Calling, calling.

Outside, it's wild.
Dad's car is stalling.
Next door my friends are
        Calling, calling.

Sliding, sledging
And, oh, snowballing!
December's pleasures
        Calling, calling.

Charlotte Lodey (9)
Alverton County Primary School
Penzance, Cornwall

STARS INSIDE
(last word)

Snowflake

I've thought of a poem.
I carry it in my hands
like a snowflake.
If it melts, I've lost it.
So I put it somewhere cold
until I can write it down.

A snowflake wouldn't
be the same without
the coldness, and
the stars inside it.

Laura Middlewick (9)
Hardford Hall County Primary School
Ipswich, Suffolk
(Age Category Winner)
(School of the Year)

Index of Titles

Index of Poets